A Day in the Life of Muffin

ISBN 979-8-88540-184-5 (paperback)
ISBN 979-8-88540-185-2 (digital)

Christian Faith Publishing
832 Park Avenue
Meadville, PA 16335
www.christianfaithpublishing.com

Printed in the United States of America

A Day in the Life of Muffin

Shirley Ann Hess Friedly

It's morning, and I'm ready to get up and start our day. I can't wait to go outside. I keep staring at Mommy, but she's not waking up. Maybe I'll help her a little bit. I'll get on the headboard and pat her on the head. It's not working, so I'll pat her a little harder. Sometimes I pat her nose. She's waking up and laughing. She thinks I'm funny.

I can't wait to get outside and sniff around the yard where the racoons and possums were last night.

I'll go over into the pasture then over to the brush pile. Maybe I'll find a mouse to play with. I love to be outside and love it even more when Mommy comes out with me. She laughs and laughs when I jump up in the air, trying to catch butterflies and bugs.

I think I'll go back in and see what special treat Mommy has for me this morning. She says, "Come on, you want your special treat?" I run to the closet, and she gets them for me. She lets me smell them, and I run to the kitchen where she gives them to me. Yummy!

Oh, good! It's time to get the mail! She says, "Mommy's getting the mail. Don't you come," because she doesn't want me down by the road. So I wait until she's coming back, then I run to meet her. I rub against her legs over and over again because every time I do, she says, "I love you too."

On our way back to the house, we play "doggie." She says, "Come on, doggie," and I trot along beside her. Sometimes I stop, and she whistles for me to come. She's so funny.

I like it when Mommy sits on the porch to pray and read her Bible. She always thanks God for me and asks him to keep me safe. It makes me feel good to know how much she loves me, and I'm so glad she's my mommy.

It's almost time for my afternoon nap. I like to take my nap on the other bed, and when Mommy walks through, I roll over on my back and stretch and look at her. She asks, "Do you want your belly patted?" She pats my belly while I fall back to sleep.

When I want to go out, I go to the back door. Sometimes there are cows in the pasture, *lots* of cows. Sometimes they are right up to the fence looking at me! They are big and look scary to me. I jump when they say, "Moo." Mommy shuts the door, and I run to the front door to go out. It's safer in the front.

Daddy has another rock pile! I love to play on the rock pile! I get on the top (Mommy calls me King of the mountain), and I knock rocks down and chase them. Mommy gets on one side and me on the other side. She says, "Peek-a-boo," and I run up to the top and peek down at her. She laughs and laughs. She is so funny. I love to make her laugh.

Here comes Daddy! I love it when Daddy comes home! I like to play with him, and he likes to play with me. He is so fun, and I love him. He loves me. He saved me when I was a little baby.

I love my aunt Sarah. When Mommy says, "Aunt Sarah is coming." I run to the window and watch for her white car. When I see it coming, I can't wait for her to get in the house so I can play with her. She calls me a miracle because she knows how bad Mommy needed me.

NASCAR
DAYTONA 500
14
OPA
OMA

My uncle Paul and aunt Alice come out for family dinners, but I love it most when they come out to watch the Daytona 500 with Mommy, Daddy, and Aunt Sarah. They try to watch the race, but I am the entertainment. They play with me and laugh at me. They always tell me bye when they leave.

I love it when Sergeant Mike, Pam, Bailey, and Logan stop by. They are patient with me as I sniff their arms and hands. They have lots of pets, and I can smell their cats and their dogs, Shooter and Carly, on them. I know Shooter and Carly because they come out sometimes.

Shoo!
Shoo!

One evening, Mommy and I were in the backyard enjoying the nice weather. I was playing on top of the swing set, and a huge bird swooped down and tried to pick me up! I jumped down just in time! It was scary! Now when big birds come around, Mommy yells, "Shoo! Shoo! Get out of here!" while she's waving her arms at them. I run under the car and watch. It is quite a sight!

I like to look out the windows, and it is really fun to look out at night to see what kind of animals might come up into the yard. I mostly see rabbits, squirrels, racoons, possums, and sometimes a deer.

When I get tired and Mommy's not ready for bed, I get in the chair by her legs and take a nap. Then when she says, "Mommy up." I get down and run to bed because I'm anxious for Mommy to pet me and rub my neck. When I'm done, I push her hand away with my back paws. Mommy thinks it's funny.

I like to snuggle up right next to Mommy in the night. Sometimes her breathing makes my ears twitch, and my whiskers tickle her nose. She pats me and says, "I love you, Muffin." I love you too, Mommy.

Winter is here. It's snowing. Mommy and I love to play in the snow. I like to dig in it and jump in it. It's soft and cold, and I have so much fun running and playing. I like to dive into the snowdrifts. Mommy watches me and can't quit laughing. She says, "Oh, Muffin, you're so funny."

Mommy said Aunt Sarah's coming to help put up the Christmas tree. I can't wait! Oh boy, a tree to climb and play with! Look at all those sparkly, glittery "toys"! Mommy calls them ornaments. Some have ribbons to chew on. I love Christmas. It makes me feel warm inside when Mommy says the best part of Christmas is that it's Jesus's birthday. Maybe her next book will be about Christmas.

Well, it's the middle of the night, and I'm dreaming about tomorrow, and all the fun things Mommy and I will do. I love my mommy, and she loves me. Mommy said God knew we needed each other, and I am so glad He put me here in my forever home.

About the Author

Shirley Ann Hess Friedly was born, raised, and has always lived in mid-Missouri. She is very thankful to God for the life that He has given her. It's a wonderful thing to be content. She was blessed with a wonderful childhood, the best parents anyone could ask for, a precious sister, and two wonderful brothers. God blessed her with one child, her beautiful daughter, Pam, who has always been the joy of her life, along with her son-in-law, Mike, and grandchildren, Bailey and Logan. In 1997, Shirley married Alan Friedly, the love of her life. With him came two more beautiful daughters, Jennifer and Michelle, and six more grandchildren, Colby, Zeth, Frankie, Malakai, Charles, and Anastasia. She gives God all the glory and praise for helping her to reach her dream of becoming an author.